Maximum Education

The Ultimate Guide to Academic Success

Steven Greene, Ed.D.
The Success Doctor

mAke the grAde

215 540 TEST
sgreene@makethegrade.net
www.makethegrade.net

Contents

Preface

"I am going to write a book." That's what I told people. Who did I tell? I told friends, my wife, students, parents of students, colleagues, neighbors, Facebook friends, and others in the education world… and when I first told people that I was going to create the book they were very excited for me. They said things like that's exciting, that's awesome, I'm sure it will be a great book, when will it be done? How do I get one? Good for you…

And then they asked, "What's the book about?

I said, "How to maximize your educational experience and study skills best practices!"

Their excitement and support and enthusiasm waned pretty quickly. Well Steve, I'm sure you can write a great book about this topic, but…

And then I would get every excuse in the book (no pun intended) not to write the book.

Aren't there thousands of books on this topic already?

It doesn't seem to be the most interesting topic in the world.
It certainly isn't a very sexy topic is it?
Isn't all this information already out there?
Isn't that stuff they already learn in school?
Isn't this mostly common sense anyway?
Can't you learn all this stuff already; why do they need another book to do it?
Even if you write a great book is anyone really going to care?
Sure, that will be good if I can't sleep…

And here's my favorite…

Who would pay attention to you?

But here's why I did it anyway.

As a teacher, educator, and private tutor for over 20 years, I have worked with over 7,000 students (and counting!!) in a wide variety of educational areas. They have ranged from third graders to adults who are going back to school in their fifties who have had just about every educational and academic challenge imaginable, but the bulk of my case load has been middle school, high school, and university students who have course level or test prep needs. We've worked on academic topics and subject matter including many levels of mathematics, the sciences, history, and writing, as well as test preparation for tests like the SAT and ACT, preparing college admissions essays, and beyond.

The one common thread that I have noticed among all students is that, on some level, they need to be systematic and organized in their scholastic processes.

They don't have a central educational study plan.

They are unable to maximize their education.

They are unable to maximize their potential.

And so, I searched around for materials to use with my students. And there were a surfeit of them. But none of them seemed to fit everyone. Learning is, after all, an individual experience, so I had to customize the materials for each student to some degree. And that is exactly what I did. In short, this book is really a compilation of what I have done and the materials and processes that I have used with the students over the years. These are the actionable tasks that work and get positive, sustainable results.

Essentially, I have compiled 20+ years of techniques, processes, and information that just plain work and get results for students at any level and in any situation.

Hence the name: MAXIMUM EDUCATION.

The goal is simple: To maximize every student's ability to get the most out of his or her education and educational processes.

You'll soon find, as you make it through the book, that there are a number of core areas that need to be addressed:
Note Taking
Outlining
Test Preparation
Time Management
Using Your Resources
Putting It All Together For A Singular, Effective Program

In the end, the information is here and available to every student. I've done my best to make it easy to understand and functional and to give you a personal escort through the technology that is available today like the Internet and the telephone. So now it's up to you – the student – to take this information, like any valuable information, and put it to its best use on a consistent daily basis.

Try it. See how it works. And let me know your feedback.

Also, keep an eye out for the sister publication – *Vocabulary: The Erudite Enigma* – which specifically addresses the area of vocabulary development, which is critical for modern students, not only in school, but in the real world.

Since education can take many forms, be sure to check out the accompanying videos, which enrich Maximum Education. They are found at: **http://www.youtube.com/powerhousesuccess,** which is my YouTube channel. You will see references to this channel throughout the book.

Lastly, who will use this manual?

Everyone!

Students
Parents
Educators

The basic principles could apply to anyone, at any grade level, if adapted or modified as needed.

My best wishes for you to maximize your education and your educational experience.

I look forward to your feedback and your success stories.

Steven Greene

"The Success Doctor"

Your Author/Instructor: Dr. Steven Greene

Dr. Greene, "The Success Doctor," is the founder and lead educator at mAke the grAde AcAdemic services, where he was helped over 7,000 success stories reach their goals. He holds a certified comprehensive science state teaching certification, as well as degrees in biology, nutrition, and psychology.

For over 20 years, he has helped his students navigate the complex world of academics, test preparation, and college admissions by teaching simple, easily applied strategies and principles that get results, improve grades and test scores, and increase confidence. He continues

to educate students and their families on a full-time basis in a Pennsylvania-based office, as well as internationally by utilizing an Internet-based classroom. His book, *Maximum Education,* is at once a hands-on workbook, a practical and useful guide for students of just about all ages, and a road map to academic success.

Be sure to check out the accompanying videos.
View the Welcome Video here:
http://www.youtube.com/powerhousesuccess.

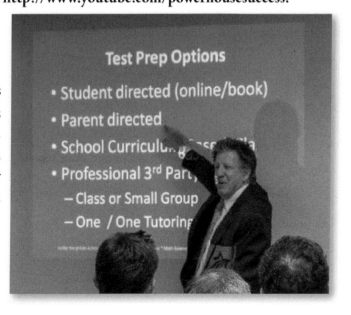

His expertise includes:

all levels of math and the sciences; as well as PSAT, SAT, and ACT preparation; study skills; and organization training. On any given day, Dr. Greene actively works with middle school, high school, and university level students (and their families) to help them to reach their goals, both inside and outside of the classroom.

So let's get started!!

Maximum Education Objectives

What do I want you to learn? Why do you want to learn?

The primary objective of this course is to provide an effective SYSTEM – a series of processes that lead from one to the next – of tools and strategies that students of all academic levels can immediately and effectively utilize to facilitate all aspects of their academic experience, both inside and outside the classroom.

This system will include strategies for:

1. Effective test-taking
2. Effective outlining
3. Effective note-taking
4. Effective tracking of short-, medium-, and long-term homework assignments
5. Time management, enabling students to plan each day/week/month
6. Prioritizing time in order to accommodate multidimensional commitments (academics, sports, extracurricular activities, etc.)
7. Increasing confidence
8. Saving time with greater efficiency in the study and academic process

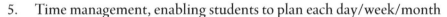

The overall long-term goal of *Maximum Education* is to develop your **CAP**:

C – Confidence

A – Attitude

P – Preparation

In other words, the **CAP** mission is:

"To develop **confidence** in one's own ability to handle the academic material through a good **attitude** that is strengthened by a consistent system of both well-planned and well-executed **preparation**."

Your day-to-day goal is simple really – to become 100% comfortable with your academic material. You will accomplish this using a series of easy-to-master processes:

1. Regular, *short dose, high frequency* exposure to the material

2. Learning and reviewing the material in a format that is similar to the way it will be presented on tests

3. Proper planning so that adequate time is available to master the material and to have all questions answered

4. Maintaining a good attitude and developing confidence in one's ability to handle situations on a test where material may not be presented in the same way or in the same words in which it was originally taught

5. Using a functional system for note-taking where the important information that is presented in class is effectively recorded

6. Using various techniques (e.g., outlining) to record important information that is learned both inside and outside of the classroom setting

7. Maintaining well-organized and functional notebooks

The final objective is to have students become independent and self-reliant in their study, which leads to consistent success.

So let's begin to develop your CAP!

Video tip: **http://www.youtube.com/powerhousesuccess**

Pre-Workbook Student Survey

Let's begin with this pre-survey. The purpose of the survey is simple: to determine where you are now so we can maximize this plan specifically for you. Simply **http://bit.ly/MTGPreSurvey** and complete the survey.

The survey is online, and the results will be processed, and you will get feedback soon, directly from Dr. Steven Greene.

BONUS: Complete the survey online, and you will get a free 15 minute consultation.

Circle your answer for each: 1 = not at all/never 5 = very much/always

Do you think you have good study skills?	1 2 3 4 5
Do you get all your homework completed on time?	1 2 3 4 5
Do you feel you are prepared for tests and quizzes?	1 2 3 4 5
Do you think you take good notes in class?	1 2 3 4 5
Are you satisfied with your ability to read and outline materials?	1 2 3 4 5
Do you feel you make the best use of your study time?	1 2 3 4 5

What are you most interested in learning in a study skills class?

_____ Note-taking

_____ Outlining

_____ Time management

_____ How to write a term paper

_____ How to study for tests

How To Best Use This Workbook

This workbook is designed as exactly that... a work book. Use it. Write in it. Take notes in it. Try to do the exercises.

There are lessons…

There are examples…

There are accompanying videos…

Develop your CAP!!

Live Course Format

This workbook is also available as a live workshop. When given live, the course consists of four 60-minute sessions. Additionally, this course is available via webinar and pre-recorded video. There are several links to videos in this workbook. Use and enjoy them.

View the welcome video here: **http://www.youtube.com/powerhousesuccess.**

Since the development of proper study skills is a practical, day-to-day process, this course is designed to be as hands-on and constructive as possible. The course will consist of a combination of examples and practice. Students will be asked to work independently, both during and outside of the class, on various processes that will facilitate and improve their learning of the study skills taught throughout the course.

Maximum Education Lessons
Course Introduction And Goals:

Lesson 1:   Homework Tracking: The Foundation

Lesson 2:   Outling Skills

Lesson 3:   Note-Taking

Lesson 4:   Putting It All Together In A Comprehensive Study Plan

Lesson 5:   What's Next?

Discuss the goals here: **http://www.youtube.com/powerhousesuccess.**

Lesson 1 –
Homework Tracking: The Foundation

What are study skills?

Study skills:

1. Include tools that a student uses to facilitate the educational process.

2. Consist of a set of processes that students use to integrate a broad range of information into manageable amounts.

3. Employ a comprehensive approach to academic material that combines note-taking, outlining, time management, and test preparation to maximize time and effort.

4. Make it faster and easier to accomplish the myriad of tasks required in an academic setting.

Why do you need study skills?

Study skills:

1. Help to manage time.

2. Increase efficiency.

3. Result in better grades.

4. Prevent "emergencies."

5. Reduce procrastination.

CASE STUDY #1: Homework Tracking High School

I began working with Dan, who was a high school sophomore. He had a typical college prep track load of courses, with a few honors classes as well. His issue, in part, was keeping track of all the assignments that he had.

> *"I get what's going on in class, but I just never feel like I am ever caught up with all of the work. Just when I get to that point, there's more work, and I feel like I am behind all over again."*

At the start, Dan's "system" was to write down all the homework in the tracking book that the school provided. Good start! He did have a good working record of what he had to do. But from there, he had no plan at all. He would start an assignment from math, and half way through it, he would shift and begin working on Spanish. Then he would move onto chemistry, etc. He was spending about 90 -120 minutes per day on homework. Once he did get done, he would put all of his completed homework into his done folder (and not into his binder area for that particular class). Since he had multiple notebooks, he would often have trouble locating the homework promptly when it was time to turn it in or go over it in class. Dan did not spent any time working ahead and anticipating longer term assignments, however. He basically only did what was due the next day.

Dan learned and started to use the Maximum Education system. He would not move onto an assignment until the present one was complete. He would file his completed work in the proper areas of his notebooks, by course. Better still, he incorporated future thinking into his daily study regimen. Over time, it worked out that he would allocate about 15 minutes per day, per class, to look ahead for future tests, quizzes, papers, and work, so he could get a head start on those as well. Within a test cycle, or about three weeks of school time, Dan improved his grades in every single course. Once he got his system in place and became consistent with it, he was spending 60-75 minutes per day on homework and study time… actually LESS than he was prior to implementing the systems… so better grades, less study time and less stress.

> *"Now that I have a system I feel like I am in control of this situation. Since I am always up to date, the subjects don't seem as challenging either. In fact, they seem to be getting easier because I really understand what's going on."*

CASE STUDY #2: Homework Tracking Middle School

"I feel like my daughter is always behind with school. When we look at her grade report, she is always missing homework assignments, which hurts her grades. How hard is it to just do the homework and turn it in?"

This is a summary of how my work with Emma began. He mother called me just after the first marking period grades posted for seventh grade. She was under the impression – based on her daughter's report at the dinner table – that all was well, and Emma's grades were fine. Now that Emma was in middle school, her parents felt that it was time for her to take ownership of her schedule and her work, so they stopped monitoring the homework as they had done in elementary school and sixth grade.

In my first meeting with Emma, she told me that, even though she wrote down the homework and did it, she didn't always get credit for it. She was spending about 45 minutes at the most on homework daily, but never on Friday or weekends ("We don't get any then," she told me). When I asked why she wasn't getting full or even partial credit, she said that sometimes teachers (she had a team of 4 teachers over her curriculum) would collect the homework, and other times, they wouldn't, and it was just bad luck that the few times she hadn't done the work were the times it had been collected. Also, she insisted the teachers hadn't given her credit for some homework she had done. When I asked why, she finally said "Well, I didn't show all of my work, and that's what the teacher wanted to see." When I asked why she hadn't shown the work, she just shrugged her shoulders and said she didn't think it mattered as long as she felt she understood the work.

In this case, our first goal was to establish a system to get the work done and done properly. The truth was the work she had done (even if incomplete) was good. It was just lacking a complete job, and she wasn't doing all the work or handing it in. So the first thing we had to do was re-establish the mindset that ALL homework is important. Frankly, whether Emma felt the homework was important or not, the teacher is the one who makes that decision in the classroom, and she needed to treat all the work with equal importance. She seemed reluctant to do this at first.

> *"If I get how to do it after 3 practice problems, then why do I have to do 30 problems for homework? That doesn't make sense to me…"*

Once we established the basic ground rules – do all homework; do all homework completely; think long term, not just about what's going on the next day in class –she was able to slowly, but surely, develop a more productive mindset. She implemented the tracking and prioritization system. She started devoting about 25% of her study time to looking to the "L" assignments. She became more diligent with her day-to-day work.

> *"I have to admit I still don't think doing the homework is the most important part of school, but it did upset me that I was getting lower grades because I didn't do it right. Since I started using the system, I haven't missed one homework assignment, and I have an A in almost all of my classes."*

CASE STUDY #3: Homework Tracking University Level

Matt was a college sophomore who was a pre-med major. He had challenging classes and was never able to get ahead of the workload. A part of the challenge at the university level (compared to the high school, middle school, or elementary levels) is that there is a constant flow of work and new information, but far fewer points of evaluation or testing. Some university classes may have only two graded events: a midterm and a final, or a paper and a final, or maybe even just a paper. Matt also had an academic history of being able to get by on his wits, and he never really had a system. Finally in this year, with this course load, he reached the overload point.

> "Before, I would just look at the material, and I would get it pretty quickly. I didn't have to take a lot of notes, and I didn't spend that much time on the homework. I just didn't need to. But this year, the volume of work has gotten to the point where I just don't know what to do first."

The first thing we did was teach Matt to use and to establish daily (even multiple times daily) attention to the homework tracking and time management system that you will also learn in this section of Maximum Education. Because the university curriculum he had at the time did not have many deadlines, we set up our own deadlines that he was to follow. We created mock test dates and other artificial events to create deadlines and checkpoints. After only 3 sessions, Matt had the system down, and he was on his way.

"I actually spend less time studying and getting organized now than I did before putting this system into place, and I feel 10x more in control of the information and the material moving ahead. It was really just a matter of following along with what I learned and doing it."

So... now... let's do it!

Tracking Homework And Daily Planning

You can't do work that you don't know you have to do.

The first step in the mAke the grAde Maximum Education study skill protocol is to always have an accurate, up-to-the-minute, and continuous record of the homework and future work that is pending.

Learn more about homework tracking at **http://www.youtube.com/powerhousesuccess**.

In short:

You must have an accurate record of your assignments and homework.

The reason should be obvious… so you know what you have to do.

But the record should and needs to be more than just a list of what is due the next day, and, as you will soon see, should include everything else that you need to accomplish.

So let's start by talking about how not to do this, just because there is pretty much an epidemic in the school population these days.

Here are some examples of how **NOT** to keep track of your homework assignments:

1. On the back of your hand
2. On scraps of paper
3. By calling or texting your friends at 10:30 at night
4. By only writing down that you have math
5. By writing down only what is due the next day and neglecting projects that are due in the near or long-term future
6. By memory
7. Not at all

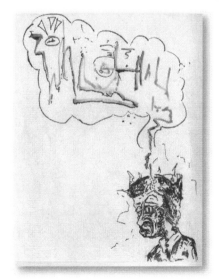

Recognize any of these techniques?

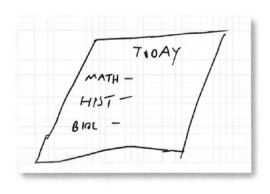

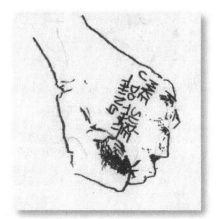

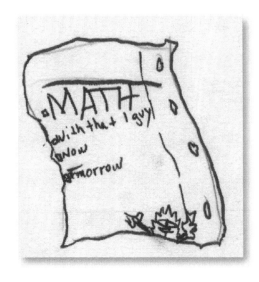

MAXIMUM EDUCATION The Ultimate Guide to Academic Success

Now, here is a much better example:

Diagram 2: good homework tracking example

DATE ____oct 14_____

MATH: PAGE 52 # 6 - 23 ODD
TRIAGLES & THEIR PROPERTIES
▲ QUIZ FRI ~ 2.1 → 23
● TEST TUES: ch 2

SCIENCE: READ/OUTLINE SECT 3.7 (CELLS)
CALL BOB ABOUT LAB DATA
TEST LATE NEXT WEEK ~ MAKE REVIEW SHEET

ENG: GREAT GATSBY READ 100~128
1ST DRAFT PAPER ON IMAGERY DUE MON
FINAL DUE 10/26

HISTORY: CONSTITUTION REPORT DUE MON
READ/OUTLINE 10.6 ON ALEXANDER HAMILTON
QUIZ THURS/FRI ~ EARLY U.S. MAP

SPANISH: VOCAB QUIZ
WORKBOOK pg 32: 1-8, 9-15 odd

Daily Planning

The first important practice in acquiring proper and effective study skills is to have an accurate daily homework plan.

This is a list of all assignments that are pending completion. Where you get this list is going to vary tremendously.

Some teachers will write the homework on a chalkboard.

Some teachers will list the homework on a web page or wikipage.

Some teachers will tell you the homework orally during the class.

Some teachers will give you a list of all the homework for a week each Monday.

Etc., etc., etc.

It is very likely, especially in the middle school level and above, that you may have multiple teachers who all have different systems.

Learn their methods, and stay on top of them!

Now, once you have your general list, the next step is to prioritize your time.

It is a 4 step process.

But first… some background jargon and abbreviations.

Prioritizing Your Time And Setting Up A Homework Agenda

Some assignments have a higher priority (**P**) than others and, therefore, need to have a special designation within the list, as do the assignments that are of less priority. The priority assigned to each assignment is based upon when it is due.

Assignments should, therefore, be defined as Short- (**S**) and Long-term (**L**).

> **S** – Short-term: Assignments due the following day
>
> **L** – Long-term: Assignments due after the following day

Once priority is designated based upon due date, the next step is to prioritize the assignments within each category (**S**, **L**) by ranking (**R**) them according to the order of importance (**1**, **2**, **3**, etc.). They are then to be completed in the order in which they are ranked.

Let's demonstrate this by example.

mAke the grAde Homework Tracking System

Use the link to download it for yourself.

Here is a template we will use to track homework.

http://bit.ly/MTGHW1Page

Here's how to use this:

Step 1: List your assignments organized by class.

Step 2: Assign the prioritization to them, S or L.

Step 3: Rank these assignments in the order that you plan to complete them. *Typically, you would complete S assignments first, then L assignments.*

Step 4: Check the D box to indicate when the assignment is done.

This is a real example for a ninth grade student who I have taught this system.

Step 1: List your assignments organized by class.

Course	Assignment	P	R	D
Math	Pg. 36: 1-13 odd, 23, 24, 25			
	Quiz Friday 10/5 on decimals (+/-/x//)			
	Test Tuesday 10/9 on chapter 2			
Biology	Outline section 3-1 on biomolecules			
	Complete section review questions #1-3			
	Lab report on compounds due Friday 10/5			
	Test on chapter 3 Monday 10/15			
English	Read book IV of the Odyssey			
	Complete study guide for book IV			
	Test on books I – IV on Wednesday 10/10			

Step 2: Give the assignments time priority.

Why was each of these assignments given the priority designation it was? The math homework on page 36 was given an S priority is because it is due the <u>next day</u>. The reason that the upcoming quiz and test are given priority L is because they occur after the next school day. These are flexible designations, but the point is to determine what has the greatest need at the moment, and then complete that assignment first.

Course	Assignment	P	R	D
Math	Pg. 36: 1-13 odd, 23, 24, 25	S		
	Quiz Friday 10/5 on decimals (+/-/x//)	L		
	Test Tuesday 10/9 on chapter 2	L		
Biology	Outline section 3-1 on biomolecules	S		
	Complete section review questions #1-3	S		
	Lab report on compounds due Friday 10/5	L		
	Test on chapter 3 Monday 10/15	L		
English	Read book IV of the Odyssey	S		
	Complete study guide for book IV	S		
	Test on books I – IV on Wednesday 10/10	L		

Step 3: Rank the assignments in the order that you plan to do them.

Notice also that we have now filled in the R column. This is a self-defined way to create your daily action plan because it determines the order that you will complete the assignments.

In this example, the student has opted to do the biology outline first, then the section review questions, then the math homework on page 36, etc. Good decisions, since these are all S assignments.

Course	Assignment	P	R	D
Math	Pg. 36: 1-13 odd, 23, 24, 25	S	3	
	Quiz Friday 10/5 on decimals (+/-/x//)	M	6	
	Test Tuesday 10/9 on chapter 2	L	8	
Biology	Outline section 3-1 on biomolecules	S	1	
	Complete section review questions #1-3	S	2	
	Lab report on compounds due Friday 10/5	M	7	
	Test on chapter 3 Monday 10/15	L	9	
English	Read book IV of the Odyssey	S	4	
	Complete study guide for book IV	S	5	
	Test on books I – IV on Wednesday 10/10	L	10	

Step 4: Check the D to indicate that the assignment is complete.

Course	Assignment	P	R	D
Math	Pg. 36: 1-13 odd, 23, 24, 25	S	3	X
	Quiz Friday 10/5 on decimals (+/-/x//)	M	6	
	Test Tuesday 10/9 on chapter 2	L	8	
Biology	Outline section 3-1 on biomolecules	S	1	X
	Complete section review questions #1-3	S	2	X
	Lab report on compounds due Friday 10/5	M	7	
	Test on chapter 3 Monday 10/15	L	9	
English	Read book IV of the Odyssey	S	4	X
	Complete study guide for book IV	S	5	X
	Test on books I – IV on Wednesday 10/10	L	10	

So let's make this clear…

Step 1: List your assignments organized by class.

Step 2: Assign the prioritization to them, S, M, or L.

Step 3: Rank these assignments in the order that you plan to complete them.
Typically, you would complete S assignments first, then M, then L.

Step 4: check the D box to indicate when the assignment has been done.

The important points to remember:

> ALWAYS complete the assignment you are working on before moving on to the next assignment.

> ALWAYS complete the assignment you are working on before moving on to the next assignment.

> ALWAYS complete the assignment you are working on before moving on to the next assignment.

Get the point?

MAXIMUM EDUCATION The Ultimate Guide to Academic Success

Try it… mAke the grAde Homework Tracking Sheet

Here is a blank tracking sheet for you to use: **http://bit.ly/MTGHW1Page**

Course	Assignment	P	R	D

Weekly Planning

The next stage of planning is on the weekly level. Weekly planning involves using a weeklong calendar to track L assignments. As you will learn in a future lesson, preparation for L assignments involves breaking the studying up into fractional, manageable units.

The weekly calendar (and the monthly calendar in the next section) greatly facilitates this level of planning. Get more calendaring tips at **http://www.youtube.com/powerhousesuccess.**
Following is an example of a weekly calendar.

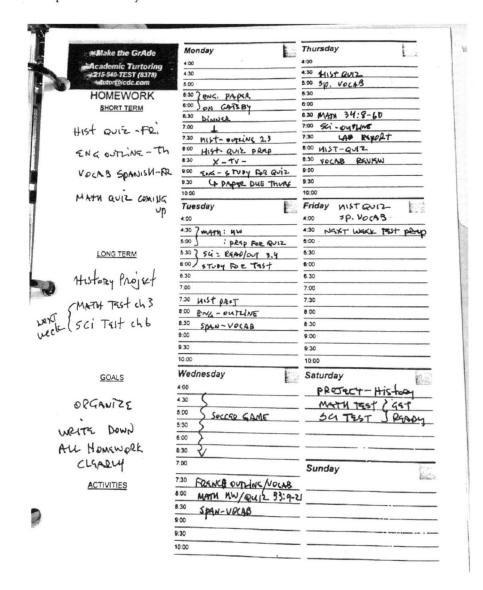

Here is a sample weekly calendar that you can use to plan:

Monday	Assignment	Goals	Activities
4			
5			
6			
7			
8			
9			
Tuesday			
4			
5			
6			
7			
8			
9			
Wednesday			
4			
5			
6			
7			
8			
9			
Thursday			
4			
5			
6			
7			
8			
9			
Friday			
4			
5			
6			
7			
8			
9			
Weekend			

Monthly Planning

The final level of planning is the monthly calendar. This enables the student to track assignments up to four weeks ahead. This is useful for both M and L assignments, but particularly for L assignments as well as major tests such as midterms and finals.

Following is an example of a monthly calendar with L assignments being tracked.

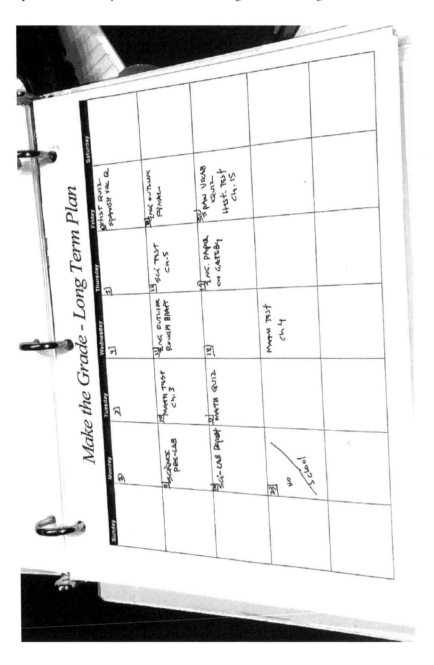

MAXIMUM EDUCATION The Ultimate Guide to Academic Success

Here is a sample monthly calendar that you can use for long-term planning:

Monday	Tuesday	Wednesday	Thursday	Friday	Saturday	Sunday

Tracking Tools

The best way to study is to complete a task before moving on to the next one.

Old School: The simplest way to track your homework would be the old school system of simply using paper and a pencil. In truth, this may actually be the best way. However, with the advent of technology, there are many other options that a student can use.

Google Drive Utilities: One of these systems is Google Drive. This is a Google (www.google.com) product, which is essentially a suite of different software products including a word processor, a spreadsheet, and many other tools. It would be quite simple to replicate the Maximum Education homework tracking system onto a Google Drive spreadsheet. The advantage of doing it this way would be portability and the ability to access the records from multiple places including your phone. These programs are also sharable, so they allow for collaboration and sharing of information. For example, I have a number of online-based (and local) students who track their home work on a Google doc and share it with me so I can monitor and see what they are doing day-to-day. Great stuff. Additionally, all Google Drive programs are free, which is a nice benefit. To find out more about using one of these programs, contact the mAke the grAde office.

Evernote: Another excellent program, which I personally use extensively, is called Evernote (**www.evernote.com**). Evernote is a program that enables the user to take notes as well as scan documents and take pictures all in one place. Even more so, it is a cross-platform product, so it can be used seamlessly on your phone, tablet, and computer, even if you have different operating systems on each. In fact, while I was writing this book, I used Evernote extensively to keep track of notes, files, and other important information that helped in the creation of the book. You can keep track of your homework by text or even by taking pictures of all sorts of things in class or outside of class, and you can put all of this into notebooks or tag it to make it searchable. It's a very versatile and robust system. There is a FREE version of Evernote, and you should start there…and if need be you may consider upgrading to their premium level (only if you need to later!). If you have questions or you would like to learn how to use Evernote, contact the mAke the grAde office.

I have only listed these two tools, but there are likely countless other ways, methods, and systems that a student or professional could use to keep track of their homework or other projects.

My advice, regardless of what you are using, is to have one system that you know works perfectly for you and your set of circumstances and get very good at using it consistently every day.

CONSISTENCY = SUCCESS = CAP

Remember:

ALWAYS complete the assignment you are working on before moving on to the next assignment.

Be sure to only do only one assignment at a time.

Never move on to the next task until you finish the task you are working on.

The last thing you should do each day is carry over any L assignments that were not completed that day to the next day's homework tracking sheet.

Now you try it… Assignment for the upcoming week:

Use the Maximum Education system to keep a detailed account of all out-of-class assignments. Use the system that we learned today to track and prioritize them.

In summary:

1. Have a detailed listing of ALL of your homework.
2. List the assignments by class.
3. Prioritize each assignment according to due date: S or L
4. Complete each assignment prior to moving on to the next one.
5. Carry over any unfinished assignments to the next day's tracking sheet.

mAke the grAde Homework Tracking Sheet Day 1

http://bit.ly/MTGHW1Page

Course	Assignment	P	R	D

Lesson 2 – Outlining Skills

Why Create An Outline?

The purpose of an outline is to condense the essential information from a large source into a smaller, more direct, and useful format.

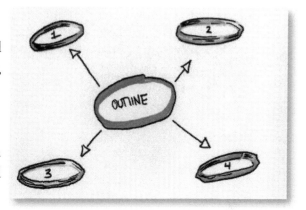

It is also to prioritize information in an organized way.

If an outline is done properly, the time that you *invest* in making your outline will pay you back over and over and save you time in the long run.

There are more outling tips at **http://www.youtube.com/powerhousesuccess.**

Once made, an outline can be used to:

1. Learn the material with the first exposure.
2. Review the material at the end of the study session.
3. Review the material for a quiz.
4. Review the material for a test.
5. Review the material for a midterm.
6. Review the material for a final.
7. Review the material to fit into context with the "big picture."
8. Create a catalog of your own notes.
9. Organize the information in the way that is most suited to you and your learning style.
10. Simplify your overall study process.

Components of a good outline:

1. Direct and to-the-point
2. Contains all essential information you need about the material you are outlining

Additionally, an outline allows you to take material from multiple sources and combine it in a single place for future reference. For example, you could combine information from class notes, the textbook, and Internet research in an outline.

What an outline does not do:

1. An outline is not supposed to rewrite the material in its entirety.

2. An outline does not substitute for reading through the original material at least once.

3. An outline does not do the work for you; it simply streamlines the process.

Class Exercise: How Do You Currently Prepare Outlines?

Think about how you have been preparing outlines up until now. Have your outlines been helping you study?

Take a few minutes and write down what you think is good about the outlines that you have been making up to this point.

Take a few minutes and write down what you think needs to improve about the outlines that you have been making up to this point.

CASE STUDY #4: Middle School Outline

Ryan was a middle school student, who I began working with midway through his seventh grade year. He was having issues organizing – specifically for science because the class involved information that the teacher provided in multiple ways such as power points, in worksheets, and also in class notes. He was having trouble integrating all this information into one singular way. "I took the information and tried to make a single outline as simply as I could, but yet it contained all the main information I needed. I was also using the outlines to organize the teacher's notes and my own notes." Ryan used the radial and line style outlines mostly because they were the most useful for this type of information and they were visual.

CASE STUDY #5: High School Outline

Organizing a term paper can be a daunting process for any high school student. Amy had to write a 16 to 20 page term paper for history class, comparing the rules and regulations of various monarchies of Europe. "Collecting and researching this information alone was a big process, but organizing it and making it useful was even harder. I was able to make different outlines for each source, while my friends were using little 3x5 cards. I used a few different outline types, but mostly the indent type and the concept maps." Amy received a 97 on her term paper, and she reported that the actual writing was the easy part because her research and other needed information was so accessible.

By the time a student gets to college, he or she has hopefully developed a strong enough skill set to process information needed at this advanced level, but he or she also needs to be able to work independently and to manage time effectively. A longtime student of mine, Dan, went off to college and quickly found that the volume of information was a challenge for him. He had learned some outlining techniques when working with me during high school, but he hadn't thought of them as organizational tools (more so a smaller scale information management usage). He connected with me asking for ways to combine the note taking techniques that he had learned with the outline skills that he has as well. "I found that each of the different types of outlines, like flow charting and circle outlining, were most effective because the information – especially in the sciences and history – tended to flow and organize in that way." He went back and redid most of his class information this way, and within a week, he told me that his workload was easier to handle and that he felt more in control of things. He also found that the outlines not only helped him to learn the material, but they also made it much easier to review and study the material when needed. "It was a great help. I knew putting the time into the outlines would reward itself multiple times because I kept coming back to them when I reviewed. And I actually enjoy making them since it makes information more visual, which helps me."

Technology Considerations

There are several common software packages that are available that make outlining as simple as typing. For example, Microsoft Word includes an "outline" screen view that allows you to automatically outline text that has been typed. Programs such as this can also produce tracking sheets (like the homework sheet from lesson 1!) and other useful forms.

There is also software, such as Inspiration, that will produce concept maps, idea maps, and other alternative forms of note-taking (which will be discussed later in the course). More recently, programs and apps have been coded specifically to help you outline. I prefer Evernote (again, as with homework tracking) for these.

How To Outline: Skim First, Outline Second

Before you start to make any outline, skim the material that you need to outline. Determine the length of the material, skim the main points, and look at any diagrams, charts or pictures that give you a fast idea of what the material is about. The outline should be the second step of the overall process.

Once you have skimmed, you are ready to make your **skeleton outline**.

Making Your Skeleton

After skimming the material, go back and make a **skeleton outline** of the major points in the reading. In the easiest case, this may be the large titles and boldfaced words that a typical science or history book provides In less obvious cases, such as a novel, you may have to assign your own headings. Considerations for outlining more general material, such as a short story or a novel, will be discussed later in this course.

When making your outline, be sure to leave space for the detailed information that will come later. Word processors are particularly handy for this. Remember, we are not concerned with detail; we are concerned with general information.

Now let's try an example. If you have ever had a biology of life science class, this will look familiar: The Structure of the Cells.

The following is an example of a **skeleton outline**:

Cells

Basic unit of life

Bordered by a cell membrane

Contain several organelles, each having a vital role in life

How cells reproduce

The skeleton outline is, in fact, useful all by itself. Quick, can you name four important things about a cell? Can you think of four topics that are certain to be on a quiz or test about cells?

The next step in the outlining process is to produce a detailed outline by filling in more information. This is what is more commonly known as outlining, but we know better now! Use the skeleton outline as a starting point, and fill in the details based upon the reading material.

Filling In The Details

The art of creating a good outline involves knowing what to include and what not to include. You need to have all the essential information – material that will certainly be on a quiz or test – and you want to leave out material that is just filler. This type of information will vary from subject to subject.

Complete the detailed outline by taking the skeleton outline and filling in information from the text beneath the headings.

The implementation of this information can take various forms: Roman numerals, letters, numbers, etc.

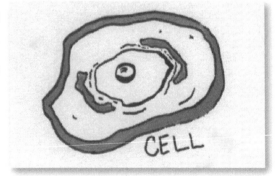

Now, here is an *example of a detailed indentation -style outline using an assortment of number/letter styles.*

Cells

1. Basic unit of life

    a. The cell theory defines the role of the cell in the living organism

    b. The cell is the most basic, smallest unit of a living thing

    c. All living things are composed of cells

2. Bordered by a cell membrane

    a. Cells, both plant and animal, are bordered by a cell membrane

    b. In addition, plant cells are enclosed in a cell wall

    c. The membrane controls what comes in and out of the cell

3. Contain several organelles each having a vital life role

    a. The cell contains several smaller units called organelles, each with an important job

        i. nucleus

            a. directs the activities of the cell

            b. controls the division of the cell

            c. controls the expression of DNA

        ii. mitochondria

            a. the site of cellular respiration and the production of energy in the cell

        iii. ribosome

            a. the site of protein synthesis in the cell

4. How cells reproduce

    a. ells reproduce by a multistep process called mitosis

    b. Mitosis is composed of 5 stages

        1. Interphase

        2. Prophase

        3. Anaphase

        4. Metaphase

        5. Telephase

    c. The duplication of DNA is done by meiosis

The Completed Outline

The completed outline is the result of filling in the skeleton outline with as much detail as you need. Remember that the outline may include more than just the material from the reading itself; you may supplement the reading with class notes or other information that you have gathered. The outline is a work in progress. You can always go back and modify it as you need to.

If you are making an outline prior to class, you may go back and add notes after the class. You can also use the outline during class to help organize your notes as the teacher lectures – there is no need to write everything down multiple times.

In the same way, you can use an outline to supplement the notes that you have already taken in class. More on this in the session on note-taking.

There are outlining tips at **http://www.youtube.com/powerhousesuccess.**

A Sample Of Good Outlining:

I. CELLS
    A. BASIC UNIT OF LIFE
        1.) Cell Theory
        2.) DALTON
    B. PARTS OF THE CELL
        1) ORGANELLES
            a. NUCLEUS
            b. RIBOSOME
            c. MITOCHONDRIA

d" outline

A Sample Of Bad Outlining:

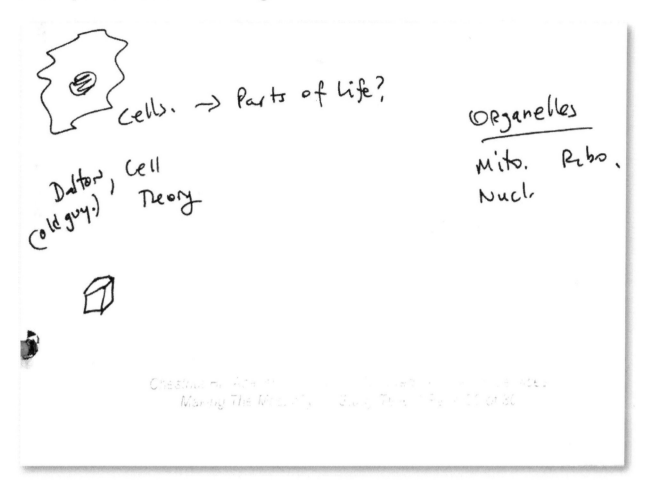

Let's look at some other more creative ways to outline… Keep in mind that different types of outlines have different uses that vary with the information that you want to outline and organize.

This is called a radial outline. You main topic goes on the inside (or hub), and the secondary topics go on the spokes of the wheel. This is basically the same core information.

Radial Outline Sample: The center circle is the main topic.

Line Outline Sample: The main topic is the center line.

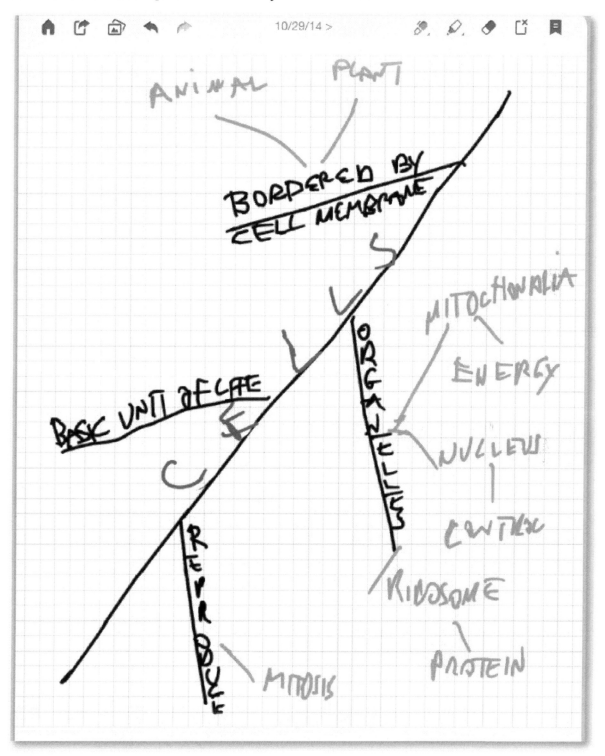

Tree Outline Sample: The main topic is the trunk.

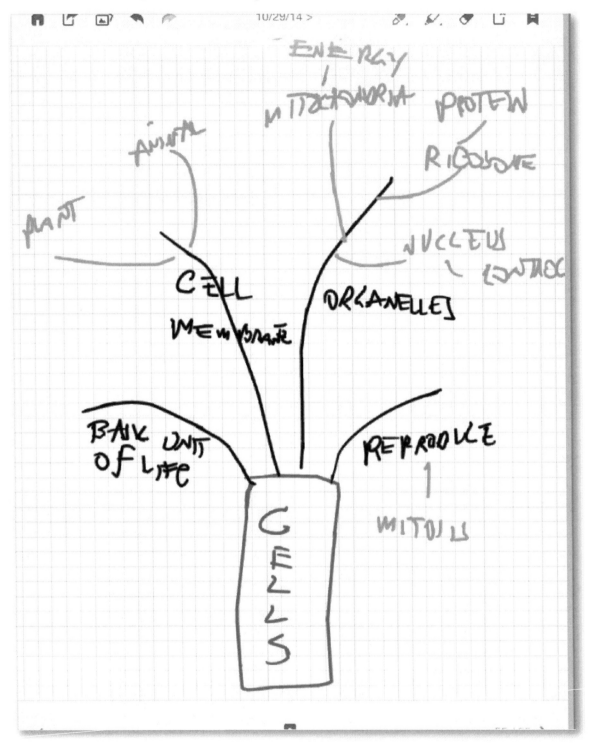

Concept Map Sample: This is more of an organizational style.

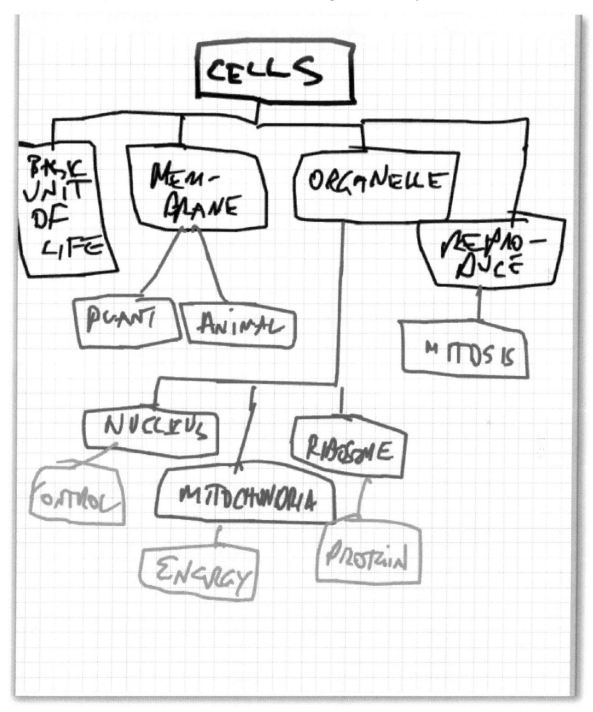

Table & Legs Sample: This is a less common style. This works better with the main ideas.

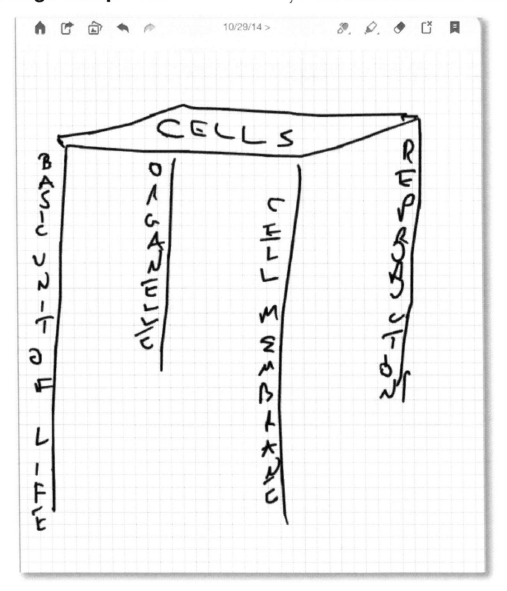

Now you try it:

Do at least one outline for each of your classes.

Concentrate on using the step method for outlining:

1. Skim
2. Skeleton
3. Detail

MAXIMUM EDUCATION The Ultimate Guide to Academic Success

Lesson 3 – NOTE-TAKING

Why Take Notes?

Your notes are your academic diary. They are your record of the information that you have seen in your classes.

The purpose of taking notes is to have an accurate record of the information that you learned in class. This is a combination of information that the teacher presents along with other discussions that may occur during a class. Considering that at the middle school, high school, and university levels you may have five or six classes at the same time, you can see the critical importance of accurate and useable notes.

As an aside, notes are not limited to schoolwork. People take notes all the time in business meetings and in many other situations… It's a life skill!

There are plenty of note taking tips at **http://www.youtube.com/powerhousesuccess.**

If you could remember everything that you heard in class (forever), you probably could get by without notes, but…

Your Notebook

What type of notebook is best?

Common types of notebooks:
Spiral Type – multiple subjects
Spiral Type – single subject
Binder (3 ring)

This is a matter of personal taste for the most part.

The big decision is whether to have one giant notebook for all of your classes, or a separate notebook for each class. The main advantage of keeping a single notebook that includes all classes is that everything is in one place. The downside is that these notebooks tend to get bulky and heavy as the year progresses. The main advantage of keeping one notebook for each individual class is that only the notebooks needed for that night's homework need to be brought home, rather than loading yourself down with an entire volume full of each class's notes. In any case, you should have a three-ring binder so you can punch holes in any handouts, papers, quizzes, tests, etc. that the teacher gives out and keep them in the notebook in neat and proper order for future use. As said before, the notebook should be your academic diary.

One tip: you can color-code new books by subject. For example, you could have all your science notebooks and folders in red and all of your math notebooks and folders in blue, and so on. Color coding is an excellent organizational system.

CASE STUDY #6: Middle School Note-Taking

When I first began working with Jennifer, a seventh grader, she was overwhelmed by the sheer load of information in all of her classes. The teachers in some classes gave a high volume of notes, while teachers in other classes relied more on handouts and PowerPoints for conveying information. Because of this inconsistency in how information was delivered, Jennifer had not developed a consistent method of cataloging and collecting information. Our solution, and one of the techniques you will see in this chapter, was to use a combination of note taking styles, primarily visual styles like flowcharts and concept maps in the classes with more information from the teacher and more two-stage note taking techniques, like the Cornell system, in classes where teachers relied on handouts and PowerPoints. Jennifer found that the combination of systems was most effective for her. She had, in the past, only had one style of note taking or outlining that she was able to use. With the addition of multiple styles and strategies, her recordkeeping became much stronger and was much easier for her to accomplish.

CASE STUDY #7: High School Note-Taking

I worked with a student named Tony who had an interesting combination of classes. He was taking two AP classes and one honors class, along with an art class and a media class. The advanced classes were often based on discussions and group projects, with less lecturing and notes given by the teacher. However, when it came time for tests and exams, a great deal of these evaluations included questions based on the discussions. Tony had the challenge of keeping track of information during the class while remaining engaged in these discussions or small group projects. We implemented a system using a combination of styles on the same outlining page that was essentially a flowchart system to cover main ideas and main topics, along with an indentation-based system that was used within many of the flowchart boxes and subdivisions. The system worked well because many of the discussions had a free-form structure to them, so the notes were not necessarily linear in the way that they were organized. However, Tony found that this combination enabled him to record the essential information in these advanced classes.

CASE STUDY #8: University-Level Note-Taking

Melanie was a university student taking business classes. She found that many of her classes were a combination of lecture information, classroom examples and what the instructor would put on the board, and practice problems that she had to do in class, typically on a worksheet. The challenge was to integrate this information into a single flowchart that enabled her to understand the important concepts. Our solution was to utilize

MAXIMUM EDUCATION The Ultimate Guide to Academic Success

technology to gather and sort information. Melanie was able to use her phone to take pictures of worked out problems the teacher had done in front of the room on the board. Once she had these pictures, she copied them into Evernote and added her written class notes as well as pictures or scans all of her worksheets and worked out problems. This use of different technologies enabled Melanie to gather, organize, and store the information in one place, which, in the past, had been separated, if recorded at all.

Class Exercise: How Do You Currently Take Notes?

Think about whatever "system" of note taking you are using now. Is it effective? Do you ever have trouble studying because your notes are incomplete or disorganized? Do you ever feel that you've underachieved on a test because you didn't have the right material to study?

Take a minute and write down what you think is good about the way you take notes now.

Take a minute and write down what you think needs to improve about the way you take notes now.

How To Decide What Is Priority Information

Like outlining, the notes you take should contain all the essentials and less of the filler. However, unlike outlining, which is done in a controlled setting (outside of class with no time constraints), note-taking is most often done in real time, while you are in class receiving a lesson.

Be aware of important elements that the teacher discusses, especially those that are written on the blackboard. Be sure that these important points are put into your notes. Ask the teacher to clarify any material that you don't understand.

Do You Have To Write Everything Down?

Notes are not intended to be a transcript of the class. You do not need to know everything that was said or discussed, just the most important information. So how do you decide what is important?

Class Exercise: What Is Important Information?

Make a short list of things that you think might be important and should be written down.

How Do You Know What Is Important?
What Should You Write Down?

The art of taking good class notes involves a combination of listening and writing. The primary way you will receive information is through listening to the teacher.

There are no hard and fast rules on how to take notes. In general, you should always write down what the teacher writes on the blackboard.

Your goal is to have an accurate and complete record of the information that you were taught during the class. You want to be sure that you are recording the important information. This leads to the question: How do you decide what information is important?

Often the teacher will begin a lecture by stating the purpose and objective for the class, e.g., "Today we will talk about the Declaration of Independence…"

Get a head start on the class… set up a template that will help to organize the information ahead of time. Here are items that you can include in your template:

Main Point:
Supporting info:
Diagrams:
Flowchart:

However, if the teacher has formally described what he or she intends to talk about, then ask yourself:

1. What is the purpose of this lecture?
2. What am I supposed to be learning?
3. What is the teacher stressing in the lecture?
4. What is the main point relating to the entire lecture?
5. What are the points that support the main point?
6. How is the lecture organized (dates, main idea, math procedure, etc.)?

The answers to these questions will define the important information in the lecture.

Try to organize your lecture notes in the same way that you would organize an outline. Get the major points down, and then fill in the details. One way to facilitate note-taking is to be prepared for the class. Did you do anything to prepare ahead of time for the class (e.g., prepare an outline, read the textbook or previous class notes, etc.)? Remember that you can take notes directly on your outline if you have prepared one. This usually saves time and reduces duplicate effort.

For a class that is primarily a visual type, like a discussion, or taught in a question-and-answer format (such as an English class analyzing a poem), you would want to take notes on the main issues that are discussed in class. These topics may emerge in a more free form manner (as opposed to those in a direct lecture by the teacher). You should listen to the main ideas that emerge in the discussions and document these.

Listening and writing at the same time is hard work!

It is difficult to listen to the teacher and write notes simultaneously. Try to develop a shorthand system if you write slowly. Here are some commonly used abbreviations:

And, also, etc.	+	**Are there any other abbreviations that you can use?**
More, greater, increase	⇑	
Less, smaller, decrease	⇓	
Therefore, causes	⇒	
Because	b/c	
With	w/	
Without	w/o	

Modifying Note-Taking For Different Courses

Different information will mandate different styles of note-taking. For example, the style you would use for history class notes will be different from the style you would use for math class. As mentioned earlier, your style of note-taking must vary depending upon the way the information is presented.

Using The Outline As Part Of The Notes

If you have an outline made ahead of time, then you already have some notes for the class. Have the outline out in front of you during the class. You can take notes directly on the outline under the existing headings or add new information to the outline as needed (in the same way you would add your class notes to the outline later).

The key here is that you don't have to reinvent the wheel. Note-taking is part of the big study picture that includes outlining, studying, and notes.

Three Alternative Note-Taking Styles

The indentation method: the common Roman numeral method

The split page Cornell method: This method involves splitting your page vertically in half. Use the left half for an outline of the material, which you completed prior to the class using material from the book. Use the right half of the page to take class notes.

A modern variation of this method is to use a PowerPoint presentation as a template for notes. Many teachers today will produce a PowerPoint for a chapter. You can print out this PowerPoint and then annotate it with your own notes.

The alternative methods (examples of these methods are shown on the following pages):

1. Radial
2. Diagonal Line
3. Flow Charts / Concept Maps
4. Pictures/Diagrams

Determining Which Style Is Best

As you become more proficient at each style of note-taking, you will be able to select the style that best suits the material presented in each class. The point is not which style of note-taking is best, but that you have more options now! As stated before, good notes are an accurate record of the important information that was taught during the class. The method that you choose to record this information should make note-taking and future review as fast and easy as possible.

Other Study Techniques:

1. Use flash cards.
2. Use pneumonic devices.
3. Create your own test questions and answer them.
4. Meet with a study buddy or a study group.
5. Practice using associative memory vs. rote memory.
6. In addition to simply reading assigned material, use a tape recorder to record yourself reading the material aloud and then play it back to yourself later.
7. Write down any questions the teacher asks in class.
8. Study in a quiet place that is free from distractions.
9. Study in regular and frequent smaller units of time, rather than fewer, longer units of time
10. Retake previous tests and quizzes.
11. Utilize online learning tools: QUIZLET
12. Utilize online organizational and sharing tools: Evernote, Google Drive documents, et al.
13. Use a voice recorder during class to record the lectures. Then you can transcribe the lectures afterward. There are a number of software programs that will do this (or just listen to them again).

Your Turn… Assignment for Week 3:

1. Be sure that you understand the main point(s) that your teachers discuss in their lectures this week.

2. Be sure that these main points are clearly recorded in your notes.

3. Outline all previous class notes prior to the next class meetings, bring the outlines to the classes, and record new notes within the outlines you prepared.

Lesson 4 – Putting It All Together: Comprehensive Study Plan

The BIG picture: How class notes and your daily study plan help you prepare for quizzes, tests, midterms, and finals

The primary goals of any study system are to complete every short-term assignment that is due each day and to prepare ahead for medium- and long-term assignments. These tasks are much easier to accomplish when broken down into consistent, smaller study periods of one or two hours at a time each day, than to complete six or seven straight hours of study in one single day.

It is the same as training for any sport: Which would better prepare you for a sports event, practicing one hour each day or seven straight hours in one day?

Check out the study plan tips at
http://www.youtube.com/powerhousesuccess.

CASE STUDY #9: Middle School Big Plan

Sarah was an eighth grade student when we began working together. She had inconsistent grades, and she complained that she was overwhelmed by her schedule and her workload. Part of this issue was the reality that she had periods of high levels of work, with some weeks having multiple tests or quizzes and other weeks having a relatively light work load. During the heavier workload periods, she was unable to keep up with the work and struggled, which resulted in sub-par grades.

She had what amounted to a grade yo-yo effect. The solution for Sarah, which is detailed in this chapter, was to break up larger projects into small daily exercises, which could be done every day. For example, knowing that she would have a history test the following week, she would study all of her history material up to that date every day (as if she had a history test the next day). The same system was utilized for each class: science, math, English, etc. Basically, she took larger projects like reports and papers and studying for tests and broke them into smaller daily activities that she found easier to complete.

CASE STUDY #10: High School Big Plan

Charlie was a high school junior in the middle of a very, very busy stretch in his academic life during the spring of his junior year. On top of this, he was planning to take college entrance exams (SATs), and he participated in sports in the spring and winter seasons. This all but insured that he did not have a lot of free time. He was taking AP world history and honors English, and the rest of his courses were college prep level courses. (This issue was a little bit like Sarah's, as they simply didn't have enough hours in the day.)

Again, the solution was multifaceted. We implemented several strategies all at once, combining outlining, note-taking, and test prep techniques, as well as chunking, blocking and time management protocols, and homework tracking and time prioritization. Charlie got the whole buffet of services! The main thing that helped him tremendously was breaking up his work into daily, manageable chunks that he was able to keep up with. The mentality was to prepare as if he was prepping for a test the next day, based on the information to date with his subjects. If he didn't have a test for six or seven days, he would study about 1/6 of that material as well as all the material up to date to that point. He found this extremely helpful. Not only was it helpful, but it was also actually more efficient. He was able to spend less time studying than he had before because he was able to use his time more effectively. Later he confided that he felt the time management calendaring was most useful because he basically understood the topics, he just wasn't able to plan things out so that things didn't start overlapping with each other and become confusing and overwhelming.

CASE STUDY #11: University Level Big Plan

Jackie had been a student at mAke the grAde throughout high school, so she was familiar with many of the study techniques, which we had learned over time. However, she didn't use all of them as effectively as she could because, frankly, she could handle the workload in high school fairly easily. Later, she went on to become a pre-med student a large university, which had a much more rigorous and demanding course load – both in terms of the time needed and the complexity of the material.

She found several things helped her in college. First of all, recording each one of her lectures, (parenthetically, many colleges and universities do this now, but at this point in time they did not), so she bought a small voice recorder and recorded all of the lectures, and then she would transcribe them later. She also made many flowcharts and concept maps because much of the information was visual, although it was taught in a text style. To prepare for tests and quizzes, and there were many of them, she studied every day for 30-45 minutes per course, to bring herself up to date on the details of each.

This study technique is called chunking or blocking, which we will talk about more in the next section. She ended up starting with somewhere between three and four hours of study time each day, which may sound like a lot, but compared to her peers, who often studied twice that amount, it was manageable. Also, and more importantly, her workflow was actually easier because she was always up to date and was able to go to the classes and lectures ready to take in any new material.

In the end, she reported that she felt that learning the skills when the pressure was off (that is to say in high school when she was able to utilize them without a lot of pressure and without a heavy overload of work) really helped her to master them. So when college time came, and it was game time, she was able to utilize many of the Maximum Education strategies in a coordinated way. As she told me, "It's so much easier when I have a system. The strategies do take some time to master, so it's better to learn them when you have the time to do it."

Putting It All Together

Let's look at a plan for preparing for the big math test on chapter 2 that is coming up in ten days. The strategy that we are going to use is sometimes called chunking. Basically, it a simple system: Break up larger assignments into smaller, more manageable ones. Think long term.

First, you should complete any short-term (**S**) assignments that are due. This applies to all subjects and is the first priority each day.

Second, look at your long-term (**L**) assignments. Divide these up into study blocks equaling the number of days that you have until the test. For example, if the test is in ten days, divide the chapter up into ten relatively equal parts (e.g., if the chapter is fifty pages, then five pages would be a tenth).

Here's an example:

The chapter consists of pages 64 to 114, or 50 pages, and we have ten days to prepare for the test. We divide the chapter up into ten smaller units and study each of them on the day allotted, as well as review the previous pages, up until the day of the test:

Day 1   64-68
Day 2   69-73 and briefly review up to that point
Day 3   74-78 and briefly review up to that point
Day 4   79-83 and briefly review up to that point
Day 5   84-88 and briefly review up to that point
Day 6   89-93   and briefly review up to that point
Day 7   94-98 and briefly review up to that point
Day 8   99-103 and briefly review up to that point
Day 9   104-108 and briefly review up to that point
Day 10   109-114 and briefly review up to that point

On day 10, in addition to the daily short-term assignments, we add another assignment: to study the last tenth of the chapter that leads up to the math test.

According to this model, on the last night before the test, if you've prepared properly, you only have to concentrate on studying the last 10% of the chapter.

This system would be applied to a test that is any number of days ahead and is especially valuable when there are two or more major assignments, tests, or papers due on the same day or within a few days of each other. By breaking up the studying of each subject into smaller, consistent, and manageable daily blocks, you will eventually have several medium- and long-term assignments in various stages of preparation. Here is an example for three subjects:

Math (test in 6 days)	Science (test in 5 days)	English (paper in 7 days)
first 1/6 of material	first 1/5 of material	set up first 1/7 of the paper
second 1/6 of material	second 1/5 of material	second 1/7 of the paper
third 1/6 of material	third 1/5 of material	third 1/7 of the paper
fourth 1/6 of material	fourth 1/5 of material	fourth 1/7 of the paper
fifth 1/6 of material	last 1/5 of material	fifth 1/7 of the paper
last 1/6 of material		sixth 1/7 of the paper
		last 1/7 of the paper

How To Study For Quizzes, Tests, Midterms, And Finals

The first task is to break the studying up into small, regular parts, as we just learned.

Your goal is to prepare for the test. This may or may not require you to simply memorize the information that you were taught. The difference is that simply memorizing the information would allow you to regurgitate it, but will it help you get the grade you want on the test?

Memorizing AND knowing the information means that you understand the information well enough to explain it in any format that the teacher asks you to on the test (multiple choice, matching, essays, etc.).

Since we are focusing on really knowing and understanding the material so as to be able to provide it in any way that the teacher might require, it makes sense to prepare for the test in the same way.

The Following are some practical study techniques:

1. Think about what information the teacher has given you about the test:
   - How long is the test?
   - How many questions are there going to be?
   - What is going to be stressed on the test?

- Are there any special cases that you have to be concerned about?
- Have you been given an essay question ahead of time?
- Do you know what types of math problems are going to be asked?
- Are there usually multiple choice questions about important dates in history?

2. Think about the important themes of the unit:

- What was the most important theme of the unit?
- What was the second most important theme of the unit?
- What was the third most important theme of the unit?

3. Make up your own test questions and practice answering them:

- Make up both short answer and essay questions.
- Try to predict the types of questions that the teacher is going to ask.
- Answer the questions that you make up.
- Use the completed test as a study guide and use it to supplement your outline (one bonus is that if you make up a practice test for each chapter of a unit, then you have a collection of them for the midterm).
- Use questions that are already available: for example, the questions from the end of the chapter or from the end of each of the chapter sections.
- See if old versions of the test are available.
- Repeat practice versions of the test more than once.
- Look for answers to questions in other parts of the test. For example, the answer to an essay question may be hinted at, or stated explicitly, in a multiple choice question.

4. Quizlet (and other online resources)

For an example see **http://bit.ly/MTG20polyatomic.**

Your Turn to Practice

Make up five short answer questions for a test that you have coming up soon.

1

2

3

4

5

Make up a practice essay question for an upcoming test.

mAke the grAde Bonus #1
Know Your Subject: Special Considerations For Different Subjects

There are many specific subject-based tips at **http://www.youtube.com/powerhousesuccess.**

Math

1. Most tests are based on completing problems similar to the ones you had in class or for homework.
2. Know all formulas and constants that the teacher will not provide on the test.
3. Show all your work – be sure that you can get partial credit whenever possible.
4. Make a single page listing every formula or process that you will need. Include examples.
5. Check your work.

Science

1. Most tests usually present a combination of short answer questions, calculations, and essays.
2. Know any important scientists.
3. Make a single page listing every formula or process that you will need. Include examples.
4. Know the major concept(s) of each chapter.
5. Review relevant vocabulary.

English

1. Most tests usually contain short answer questions about details.
2. Study important quotes.
3. Know the main characters.
4. Understand the plot line.
5. Review important vocabulary.
6. Exams almost always include essays about major concepts or characters.

History

1. Most exams usually contain a short answer section about people/places/dates.

2. Make a list of people and the most important thing that each did.

3. Make a timeline of important events and dates.

4. Know important laws or significant events (treaties, etc.).

5. Most tests require essays.

6. Study any special vocabulary.

Foreign Language

7. Tests usually concentrate on vocabulary and grammar.

8. Understand the culture of the country if you have studied it.

mAke the grAde Bonus #2:
Organizing A Term Paper

1. Choose a topic (if one is not assigned):

    -   Not too broad or too narrow
    -   Be clear on what you are going to research and write about before you start.
    -   Define your thesis with a thesis statement.

2. Consider your sources:

    -   textbooks
    -   teachers
    -   library
    -   internet – search engines and key words
    -   magazines & newspapers
    -   encyclopedias & almanacs & yearbooks
    -   videos
    -   specialists in their field
    -   Library of Congress

3. Set up an agenda:

    -   Papers are usually long-term (**L**) assignments.
    -   They have intermediate deadlines, for example:
        3/7 – thesis statement due
        3/10 -- first draft due
        3/17 – list of five sources to be handed in
        3/24 – final draft due
        3/31 – completed paper due

4. Compose the first draft:

    -   Don't worry about getting it right; just get it down.
    -   Develop your topic using a variety of sources.
    -   Work in small units, concentrating on one section at a time.

5. Revise for the final draft:

    -   Be sure to proofread, checking all spelling and grammar.
    -   Be sure that you have answered your thesis question.
    -   Does the paper flow? Does each paragraph pick up where the previous one left off and lead to the next paragraph?
    -   Work in small units, concentrating on one section at a time.
    -   Rewrite as needed.

6. Prepare the final draft:

    -   Include a title page.
    -   Include a bibliography.
    -   Proofread your work.
    -   Remember that neatness and presentation count.

mAke the grAde Bonus #3:
Preparing For Standardized Tests: The PSAT, SAT, And ACT Exams

The goal is to become 100% comfortable with the information through:

1. Regular, short dose, high frequency exposure to the material.

2. Learning and reviewing the material in a format that is similar to the way it will be presented on the test.

3. Proper planning so that adequate time is available to master the material and to have all questions answered.

4. Maintaining a good attitude and developing confidence in your ability to handle situations on a test where material may not be presented in the same way or in the same words in which it was originally taught.

There are several strategies within the tests that include:

SAT
Reading
    Sentence Completions
    Short Reading
    Long Reading

Math
    Multiple Choice
    Grid In Questions

Writing
    Essay
    Multiple Choice
        Sentence Improvement
        Sentence Corrections
        Improving Paragraphs

ACT
    English
    Math
    Reading
    Science
    Essay

There is PLENTY of test prep information at **http://www.youtube.com/powerhousesuccess.**

mAke the grAde Bonus #4:
Different Styles Of Learning AND Teaching: How Do YOU Learn Best?

There are three distinct styles of learning:

1. Visual – you learn best by seeing something.

2. Auditory – you learn best by hearing something.

3. Kinesthetic – you learn best by doing something.

Very few people are purely one style. Most people are a blend of all three, or people learn different types of information through different styles, depending upon the subject. For example, you may learn science best by observing it visually, while math you learn best through the kinesthetic style (actually doing the problems).

Class Exercise: Learning Styles

Which learning style are you?

Different Styles Of Teaching

Similarly, these three distinct styles can be applied to teaching: Subjects can be taught using either the visual, auditory, or kinesthetic style. Try to be aware of your teachers' styles. If a teacher's style of teaching differs from your optimal style of learning, you may have to adjust to your teacher's style.

Class Exercise: Teaching styles

What style does each of your teachers use?

MAXIMUM EDUCATION The Ultimate Guide to Academic Success

How To Continually Improve

Always look ahead.

Planning is the key to success.

Plan each day, each week, and each month.

Every day, update your homework and study plan to accommodate any new assignments, and record the assignments that you have completed.

This is a process. The expectation is not that you will suddenly wake up tomorrow and be the perfect note taker or the perfect example of time management and outlining. But the expectation is that you now have a roadmap to improvement and to steadily and consistently work toward your goals.

Academic success is no different than any other pursuit. It takes time and commitment and focus. If you want to play the guitar, you play and practice your guitar every day. It's the same with academics. It is a daily process. But it doesn't have to be difficult. You just have to be CONSISTENT!

Trust me, the more you work on this, the easier it gets!!!

Some people like to be very analytical about their progress, and others are more random. Generally, the most common metrics of academic success are grades and test scores. Of course these are important. But there are many other gauges of success: confidence, attitude, preparation, time management, lack of stressful situations, the ability to keep up with challenging classwork because you are prepared, and on and on. Try not to focus only on grades, but consider the bigger picture.

Finally, there are countless ways to determine success. It is up to you to define that for yourself and to make it happen for yourself.

What's Next?

Your study plan is something that you are always working on and trying to improve.

It is very much an evolving process. And it will change for both internal (your skill set) and external (what classes you are taking, what your goals are, etc.) over time.

Check out these videos: **http://www.youtube.com/powerhousesuccess.**

So be realistic: Concentrate on improving one aspect at a time. Work on that aspect until you have mastered it, then move on to the next one. For example, work on outlining until you have mastered it, and then move on to note-taking.

Make your study and Maximum Education process a *habit*.

And… know that there are people available to help you.

We at mAke the grAde are here to help you.

Join the mAke the grAde community Facebook page at this link: **www.facebook.com/MTGrade.**

This is set up specifically to help you/your family with your Maximum Educational questions and areas of need. You can share stories and interact with others in the group.

If you find you have questions, make sure that you ask for answers and are then satisfied with your understanding of the material; if you aren't, keep asking until you are.

Ask for help when you need it. Take advantage of the resources you have.

And use your time wisely.   Form a study group.

Your parents and your teachers are also there to help.

The final goal is to become independent and self-reliant in your studies and all aspects of your life. Escapes persists

Organization is not limited to academics; these skills are helpful in all aspects of your life.

Remember, the overall long-term goal is to develop CAP:
> **C – Confidence**
> **A – Attitude**
> **P – Preparation**

"To develop **confidence** in one's own ability to handle the academic material through a good **attitude** that is strengthened by a consistent system of both well-planned and well-executed **preparation**."

What Do You Think?
Student Survey

http://bit.ly/MTGPostSurvey

	1 = not at all/never	5 = very much/always
Did the workbook help you?		1 2 3 4 5
Will you use the techniques that you learned in this class?		1 2 3 4 5
Did you do your homework?		1 2 3 4 5
Did you find the class interesting?		1 2 3 4 5
Did you like the instructor's presentation?		1 2 3 4 5
Would you like to have another follow-up class in the future?		1 2 3 4 5

What did you learn in the class that will help you the most?

What did you learn in the class that will not help you at all?

What would like to have learned more about?

What do you think was covered too much?

What did you think of the Study Skills class in general?

Questions about the survey?
Go to: **http://www.youtube.com/powerhousesuccess**

What the parents and students   say...

"I used Dr. Greene's services when my son was in 11th grade when he got a not so good SAT score. We had signed on to another SAT class situation which wasn't helping and that was a waste of time and money. We decided to go for Dr. Greene's private tutoring. In a matter of weeks with Dr. Greene's system of powerhousing he was able to raise his score significantly. Dr. Greene is great with teenagers with an unassuming manor that puts them at ease all the while with the ability to say the right things to help them along to their goals. I highly recommend his services and his advice in marketing and educational services ."
Jane L. (parent)

"As an educator and advisor of high school students pursuing a college career, I find that most students have so much going on that they lose track of how to prioritize. This useful handbook gives students of all ages and grades the tools necessary to succeed in all subject areas. Strategies for note taking, outlining, and studying are presented using examples that students can mirror in their own classwork. Dr. Steven Greene is practical, knowledgeable, and uses common sense approaches to help students organize themselves for life-long learning. I would recommend this handbook for my own clients, as well as those looking for quick advice that they can implement into their lives NOW!"
Cheryl DiLanzo, M.S. Montgomery County Community College/ACE College Advising.

"Dr. Steve Greene to the rescue. If it sounds like he is a hero, indeed this is true. If you have a son or daughter who needs testing or subject matter help, Steve will step up with all his wisdom, heart, and soul. He is extremely knowledgeable and understanding of the mindset of teenagers and individualizes his teaching methods for each student. In addition to improving test taking and scores, the most amazing feat Steve performed was to connect with our son's chemistry teacher. He drove to the high school and figured out exactly where the "learning gaps" in class and homework existed. In our son's words, "He went out of his way to ensure success with a teacher and class I was struggling with. I am a better person and student because of Steve Greene."
David Kale, Kale Design (parent)

"Steve is a great help to my children when they have difficulties with math. He is always willing to fit them into his schedule and work around their other activities. His knowledge of math, ability to connect with children, and willingness to work around our busy schedules makes him the perfect choice for a tutor."
Sandy S. (parent)

"Steve has a wonderful ability to hone in on what the student's academic and emotional needs are, while helping to maximize their potential. He is incredibly patient and focused while working one-on-one and helping the student understand and learn the material. Steve is incredibly accepting of the craziness of teenagers' schedules and working around their schedules to fit in tutoring time. Our family is fortunate to have the opportunity to work with Steve."

Andrea R. (parent)

Dr. Greene is tutoring my daughter for chemistry. I was a little skeptical about online tutoring, but Dr. Greene has been most helpful. Using the whiteboard online allows my daughter to watch him write out the formulas. We have partnered with a friend, and both girls can work together with Steve from our own homes. Steve is easy to talk to, flexible with scheduling, and will make you feel comfortable and secure about what you are learning. I feel relieved that we have a quality resource for chemistry and physics, as I am no help at all!"

Rebecca W. (parent)

"Dr. Greene has tutored both my son and daughter for various levels of math. He was able to adjust his methods and teaching styles to best suit their individual needs and was successful in helping them improve their grades. I would also note that Dr. Greene works with a flexible schedule to accommodate the kids' various activities and responsibilities."

Vivian M. (parent)

"Steve is a great math tutor. He helped me reach my target GRE score an a little over a month-and-a-half of bi-weekly tutoring. The online format is PERFECT for a busy working mom like me. What makes Steve's tutoring unique is that it is 100% tailored to your needs, not what a set curriculum or some course designed. He is open and engaging as well. If you are looking for a great math tutor, Steve is the man!"

Susan C. (student)

"Steve utilized his follow-up skills to make sure our appointment was confirmed. He is courteous and understanding to your needs. He informed me, prior to the meeting, of the questions he had prepared to ask and also informed me of the timeframe needed to complete the audio interview. I felt very comfortable during the interview because I was informed of the process. It was an overall good experience."

Annamarie S.(student)

"Steven Greene tutors our son, who is a junior in high school. His teaching style, especially in chemistry and physics, helped our son grasp the information with ease. We also have Steven going over SAT strategies to prepare for the upcoming test. From a parent's point of view, Steven is very professional; can relate to our son; is always available by phone or email, if needed; and after each session, updates us with what material he went over and the progress our son is making."

Lisa Y. (parent)

"Dr. Green tutored my son for the SATs and helped him to raise his scores dramatically when classes had failed. He has a wonderful way with teens and puts them at ease. He shows how to study for the SATs in an effective way. The scores matter."

Jane L. (parent)

Get Connected... to the Success Doctor

mAke the grAde
sgreene@makethegrade.net or **http://www.makethegrade.net**

Schedule a 1:1 appointment:
http://bit.ly/MTG60 <<60 minute session
http://bit.ly/30MTG30 <<30 min session
http://bit.ly/15mtg15min << 15 min session

ONLINE COMMUNITIES

Share ideas, communicate with Dr. Greene and the rest of the community. Get real time tips and information. Post your successes. Ask questions. Engage!

Facebook:
http://www.facebook.com/mtgrade

Linkedin:
http://www.linkedin.com/in/makethegrade

Twitter:
http://www.twitter.com/makethegrade

Instagram:
http://www.instagram.com/makethegrade

Thank you!!!

Have a Powerhouse day!!

Check out the Thank You video at **http://www.youtube.com/powerhousesuccess.**

Made in the USA
Middletown, DE
12 March 2020